WORLD IN
FOCUS

FOCUS ON
Afghanistan

NIKKI VAN DER GAAG

WORLD ALMANAC® LIBRARY

Please visit our web site at: www.garethstevens.com
For a free color catalog describing World Almanac® Library's list of high-quality books
and multimedia programs, call 1-800-848-2928 (USA) or 1-800-387-3178 (Canada).

Library of Congress Cataloging-in-Publication Data available upon request from publisher.

ISBN 978-0-8368-6748-0 (lib. bdg.)
ISBN 978-0-8368-6755-8 (softcover)

This North American edition first published in 2008 by
World Almanac® Library
A Weekly Reader Corporation imprint
200 First Stamford Place
Stamford, CT 06912 USA

Commissioning editor: Nicola Edwards
Editor: Patience Coster
Inside design: Chris Halls, www.mindseyedesign.co.uk
Cover design: Wayland
Series concept and project management by EASI-Educational Resourcing
(info@easi-er.co.uk)
Statistical research: Anna Bowden
Maps and graphs: Martin Darlison, Encompass Graphics

World Almanac® Library editor: Alan Wachtel
World Almanac® Library cover design: Scott Krall

Picture acknowledgments. The author and publisher would like to thank the following for allowing their pictures to be reproduced
in this publication:
CORBIS 8 (Stapleton Collection), 9 (Mimmo Jodice), 13 (Rahmat Gul/epa), 15 (Francois Carrel/Montagne Magazine),
17 (Reuters), 19 (CORBIS Sygma/Patrick Robert), 20 (Michael S. Yamashita), 22 (Ron Sachs/CNP), 24 (epa), 25 (David Bathgate), 26
(CORBIS Sygma/Silva Joao), 27 (CORBiS Sygma/Christian Simonpietri), 28 (Stephanie Sinclair), 33 (Adrees Latif/Reuters), 34 (Reuters),
47 (David Bathgate), 49 (Ahmad Masood/Reuters), 56 (DLILLC), 59 (Syed Jan Sabawoon/epa); EASI-Images/Jenny Matthews 4, 5, 6, 10,
11, 12, 14, 16, 18, 21, 23 and *title page*, 29, 30, 31, 32, 35, 36, 37, 38, 39, 40, 41, 42, 43, 44, 45, 46, 48, 50, 51, 52, 53, 54, 55, 57, 58.

The author would like to thank Ali Askari for his research.

The directional arrow portrayed on the map on page 7 provides only an approximation of north.
The data used to produce the graphics and data panels in this title were the latest available at the time of production.

Printed in China

1 2 3 4 5 6 7 8 9 10 09 08 07

CONTENTS

Cover: Women taking an adult literay class in Hesarak village in northern Afghanistan.

Title page: A meeting to elect members of the Loya Jirga, or Grand Council, takes place in Mazar-e Sharif in December 2003.

CHAPTER 1

Afghanistan – An Overview

Afghanistan is a mountainous country in central Asia. In the most recent episode of its turbulent history, Afghanistan's people have experienced 27 years of war and their troubles are not yet over. Afghanistan is famous for having been ruled by a regime known as the Taliban, which enforced its own strict version of Islam and sheltered the Islamic fundamentalist leader Osama bin Laden from 1996 to its fall in 2001.

A STRATEGIC POSITION

For the people of Afghanistan, the Taliban were simply the most recent in a long line of rulers and conquerors. For centuries, control of Afghanistan has been regarded as essential for the domination of the whole of central Asia. Many people have risked their lives traveling the treacherous routes through Afghanistan's high mountain passes to battle for conquest of the country. Afghanistan's strategic position—it lies along the ancient "Silk Route," and it is sandwiched between the Middle East, central Asia, and the Indian subcontinent—made the prize worth the difficult journey for Genghis Khan, Alexander the Great, the Persians, the British, and the Soviet Union.

▼ People walk past one of the Bamiyan Buddhas in 1998, before the Taliban destroyed the Buddhas.

▲ Young women attend a tailoring class in Ufimalik village. Projects such as this help give people the opportunity to find work and avoid poverty.

Afghanistan has a rich culture dating back thousands of years. It is home to the remnants of the huge 2,000-year-old Bamiyan Buddhas that were destroyed by the Taliban in 2001. It was the birthplace of Zoroaster, who founded the Zoroastrian fire religion, and home to poet-philosopher Jelauddin Rumi (1207–1273) and the famous scientist and philosopher Avicenna (980–1037).

RICH AND POOR

Afghanistan is a country rich in resources as well as history. It has gems, gold, copper, coal, iron ore, gas, and oil. It is also a country with many different ethnic groups; the main ones are the Pashtun, Hazara, Tajik, and Uzbek. More than 30 languages are spoken in the country.

Many of Afghanistan's resources have only been discovered since the 1960s. The country's terrain, climate, and years of war mean that few have been extracted. Instead, there has been a thriving trade in opium poppies. Afghanistan is the world's largest producer of opium, from which the drug heroin is made. It is also one of the poorest countries in the world. Its average life expectancy today is only about 43 years, and one child out of four dies before the age of five.

Twenty-seven years of war and repression have left the country's infrastructure badly damaged, its economy in tatters, and its people living in poverty. Frequent breaks in the delivery of the power supply, even in the capital city of Kabul, make daily life difficult. Afghanistan is a dangerous country to live in, and many areas are troubled by the return of Taliban fighters. The Afghans are a proud and resilient people, but improving their lives and setting their country on the road to a better future will not be easy.

Physical Geography

- Land area: 250,000 sq miles/647,500 sq km
- Water area: 0 sq miles/0 sq km
- Total area: 250,000 sq miles/647,500 sq km
- World rank (by area): 42
- Land boundaries: 3,436 miles/5,529 km
- Border countries: China, Iran, Pakistan, Tajikistan, Turkmenistan, Uzbekistan
- Coastline: 0 km/0 miles (landlocked)
- Highest point: Noshaq (24,558 ft/7,485 m)
- Lowest point: Amu Darya (846 ft/258 m)

Source: CIA World Factbook

 Did You Know?

Afghanistan is one of the most heavily mined countries in the world. There are landmines in all but two provinces, most of them laid during the time when the Soviets occupied the country. There are many people who have had their arms and legs blown off as a result of stepping on landmines.

▲ A woman walks along a road through a heavily landmined area near Bagram. The marker stones show the safest way through the minefield.

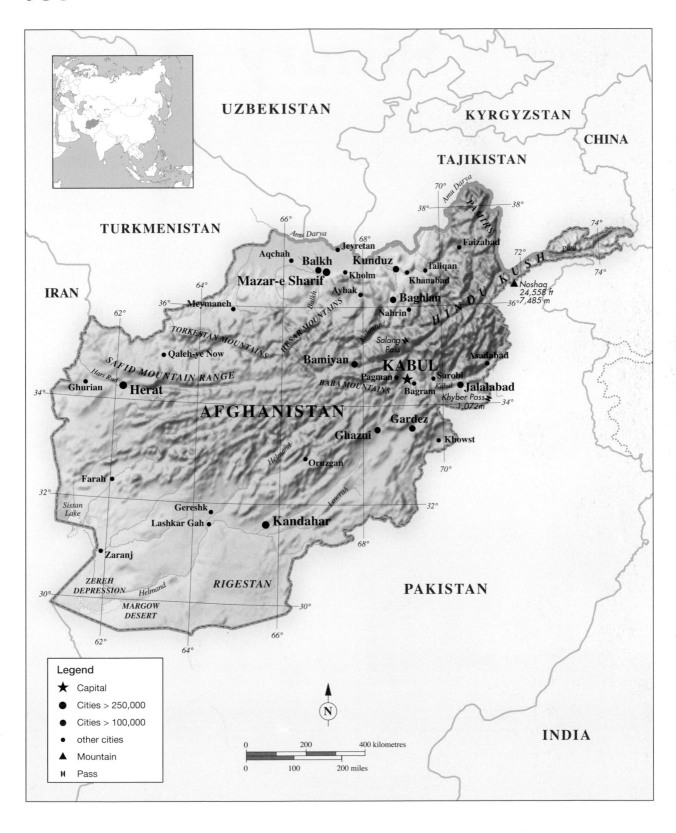

UZBEKISTAN

KYRGYZSTAN

CHINA

TAJIKISTAN

TURKMENISTAN

70°

38°   38°

Amu Darya

PAMIRS

66°   68°

74°

Faizabad

72°

Panj

IRAN

Aqchah   Jeyretan

Kunduz

Taliqan

74°

Balkh

64°   Kholm   Khanabad

Mazar-e Sharif   Aybak

Noshaq
24,558 ft

36°   Meymaneh

62°

Baghlan

36° 7,485 m

Amu Darya

Balkh

Nahrin

HINDU KUSH

TORKESTAN MOUNTAINS

HESAR MOUNTAINS

Kunduz

Salang
Pass

Qaleh-ye Now

SAFID MOUNTAIN RANGE

Bamiyan

KABUL

Asadabad

Hari Rud

Pagman

Sarobi

34°   Ghurian

Herat

BABA MOUNTAINS

Bagram

Kabul

Jalalabad

Khyber Pass

AFGHANISTAN

Gardez

1,072 m   34°

Ghazni

Khowst

Helmand

Oruzgan

70°

Farah

32°

*Sistan
Lake*

Gereshk

Lowrah

32°

Lashkar Gah

Kandahar

68°

Zaranj

*ZEREH
DEPRESSION*   *Helmand*

RIGESTAN

PAKISTAN

*MARGOW
DESERT*

30°

30°

62°

64°   66°

INDIA

Legend

★ Capital

● Cities > 250,000

● Cities > 100,000

• other cities

▲ Mountain

)(Pass

N

0		200		400 kilometres

0	100	200 miles

CHAPTER 2

History

As a result of its strategic location, Afghanistan has been a battleground for the many peoples who have struggled for possession of its mountainous terrain.

ANCIENT AFGHAN EMPIRES

People have been living in Afghanistan since 5,000 B.C. The region became part of the Persian Empire when it was conquered by Darius the Great (521–486 B.C.). In 329 B.C., the Macedonian military commander Alexander the Great (356–323 B.C.) ousted the Persians. Reminders of his rule are still found today. Many towns in the country, for example, are built on Greek foundations.

From the first century A.D. to the middle of the fifth century A.D., a Buddhist civilization ruled the ancient kingdom of Gandhara, which stretched from eastern Afghanistan to northwest Pakistan. Buddhist art and culture reached its peak with the accession of King Kanishka (A.D. 100–144). Buddhist kings reigned in the city of Bamiyan, in the heart of the Hindu Kush mountains, until the tenth century.

In 962, invading Arabs began the Ghaznavid dynasty and introduced Islam to the country. In the thirteenth century, Afghanistan was conquered by the Mongolian warrior Genghis Khan (c. 1162–1227). Khan conquered most of central Asia, including lands that are now Afghanistan, Tajikistan, Uzbekistan, and Turkmenistan, and moved westward into what is now Turkey. In 1273, the Venetian merchant Marco Polo crossed Afghanistan on his voyage from Italy to China and discovered the Silk Route, which had once been the main route between Europe, the Near East, India, and China.

In 1370, the Mongolian warrior Tamerlane (c. 1336–1405), who claimed to be descended from Genghis Khan, became the next in a long line of conquerors. His descendants continued

Did You Know?

Tamerlane was called "Timur the Lame" by Europeans because he walked with a limp. His leg had been injured when he was a child.

◄ A painting from an old manuscript shows Genghis Khan outside his tent.

◄ An ancient mosaic of Alexander the Great, who drove the Persians out of Afghanistan in 329 B.C.

to rule the area until the Persians took over in 1550. They also founded the Moghul Empire in India. The next two hundred years saw constant warfare with Persia. In 1750, King Ahmad Shah Abdali established the Kingdom of Afghanistan. At its height, this kingdom stretched from the city of Delhi, in the east, to the Arabian Sea, in the south.

Focus on: The City of Balkh

Balkh, the oldest city in Afghanistan, is known locally as the Mother of Cities. Originally called Bactria, its origins date back many thousands of years, and it has been home to Buddhists, Jews, and Muslims. Zoroaster, founder of the Zoroastrian religion of fire, is said to be buried in Balkh, and the philosopher-scientist Avicenna was born there in 980 A.D. Balkh was sacked twice: by Genghis Khan in 1220, and by Tamerlane in the fourteenth century.

THE NINETEENTH CENTURY

In the nineteenth century, Afghanistan became involved in a rivalry between Britain and Russia, both of which wanted control of the country. Between 1839 and 1842, Britain fought the Afghans in what became known as the First Afghan War. Britain installed Shah Shuja as a puppet king, but he was assassinated in 1842. The Afghan leader, Dost Mohammed Khan, drove back the British forces and declared himself king. The war ended in disastrous defeat for Britain.

In 1878, in the Second Afghan War, Britain backed a new king, Abdul Rahman Khan, who remained on the throne until his death in 1901. Britain withdrew from Afghanistan but continued to control its foreign affairs and supply arms. In 1893, the Durand Line fixed the borders of Afghanistan and British India, splitting up Afghan tribal areas and leaving many Afghans in what is now Pakistan.

INDEPENDENCE

In 1919, following World War I, increasing numbers of Afghans wanted independence from Britain. The Afghan king, Habibullah, was assassinated because of his support for Britain. His son, Amanullah Shah, then declared independence. This was immediately recognized by Russia and, after a month of fighting—the Third Afghan War—by Britain. Amanullah Shah instituted reforms, but they were controversial, and he was forced to abdicate in 1928. In 1930, Nadir Khan took the throne and continued some of the reforms, but he was assassinated in 1933. His son, Mohammed Zahir Shah, succeeded him and went on to develop a constitutional monarchy and tried to modernize the country. In 1959, women were allowed to enroll in universities and to take jobs outside the home. In 1973— with the Soviet Union's support—Zahir Shah's cousin, Daoud Khan, staged a coup, proclaiming the country a republic and himself president.

THE SOVIET UNION INVADES

In 1978, Daoud was killed in a coup staged by the communist People's Democratic Party of Afghanistan (PDPA). Party chief Nur Mohammed Taraki became president and signed a treaty of friendship with the Soviet Union. At the same time, the Afghan guerrilla movement was born. Its members were known as the mujahideen, a word that has been used more generally since that time for those who fight for an Islamic cause. In 1979, the Soviet army invaded Afghanistan and massacred hundreds of peasants. The mujahideen started to attack the Soviet troops and, in the fighting that followed, both the U.S. ambassador and Taraki were killed. The previously exiled communist leader Babrak Karmal took power.

▼ A young girl stands in front of a wrecked Soviet tank in Kabul in 1996. The war between the Soviet Union and the mujahideen destroyed many buildings in the city.

▶ Young women from a local militia organized by the Soviet Union to fight the mujahideen pose with their weapons.

The Soviets feared that the United States would attempt to assert its influence in Afghanistan. Therefore, in December 1979, the Soviet government sent in troops to fight the mujahideen and support Karmal. There was nationwide resistance to the Soviet invasion. Tens of thousands of mujahideen were trained in Pakistan and funded by the United States, Saudi Arabia, and China. The U.S. Central Intelligence Agency (CIA) began giving aid covertly to the mujahideen. Millions of Afghans fled to refugee camps in Pakistan. Soviet forces controlled the country's government and resources and bombed the countryside, killing thousands of people and destroying villages.

From 1980 to 1986, the CIA provided U.S.$2 billion in military aid to the mujahideen, who were also funding their war through the opium trade. U.S. president Ronald Reagan's National Security Decision Directive 166 called for efforts to drive the Soviets from Afghanistan

"by all means available." In 1987, Mohammed Najibullah, head of Afghanistan's secret police, was installed as president. Finally, under an agreement signed in Geneva, the Soviet army withdrew in 1988. About two million Afghans had lost their lives and six million had been made refugees. Also, fifteen thousand Soviet troops were killed in the confict.

THE FIGHT FOR KABUL

Despite the Soviet withdrawal, fighting in the country continued. Many people were opposed to Najibullah. Different warlords controlled different areas of the country, and they were supported by different foreign backers. Afghanistan was breaking apart, and the United Nations (UN) failed to get the various sides to agree. In 1992, the four main factions of warlords—Dostum, Massoud/Rabbani, Hekmatyar, and Hizb-i-Wahdat—fought for control of Kabul, the country's capital. About one million fled the city, 20,000 were killed, and many became refugees.

ENTER THE TALIBAN

In 1994, a new force known as the Taliban was born in Afghanistan. Many of its leaders were mujahideen who had formerly been funded by the West to drive the Soviet Union from their country. The Taliban took over the cities of Kandahar and Herat before capturing Kabul and executing Najibullah in 1996. Its members were driven by a strict version of Islam. They imposed Sharia on the country, banning women from working or going outdoors without a man, and forcing them to dress in an all-encompassing garment called the burqa. They closed girls' schools and insisted that all men grow beards. They banned television, music, and art and destroyed many ancient treasures, including the Buddhas of Bamiyan.

In 1998, U.S. cruise missiles were fired at alleged terrorist training camps in Afghanistan. The United States said that this was retaliation for the destruction of American embassies in Kenya and Tanzania by local members of an Islamic organization called Al-Qaeda whose leaders were based in Afghanistan. Iran sent thousands of troops to its Afghan border, and threatened to invade to stop the Taliban's "ethnic cleansing" of Afghanistan's Shi'a Muslim minority. By 2000, the Taliban controlled about 80 percent of Afghanistan. Only Pakistan, Saudi Arabia, and the United Arab Emirates recognized the Taliban as a legitimate government.

In 2001, the Taliban tortured and killed hundreds of Hazaras in Yakaolang. In the same year, the military leader Ahmad Shah Masoud of the Northern Alliance—a force made up of those in Afghanistan opposed to the Taliban—was killed by suicide bombers posing as journalists.

▼ This is what women under the Taliban saw through their burqas, which covered them from head to toe with only a small gap to look through. Some women in Afghanistan still wear the burqa.

▶ In September 2005, a woman from Jalalabad votes in the country's National Assembly elections.

SEPTEMBER 11 AND THE INVASION

On September 11, 2001, four airplanes were hijacked by 19 terrorists. Two of the planes were deliberately flown into the World Trade Center in New York City; a third was flown into the Pentagon, in Washington, D. C.; and the fourth crashed into a field after passengers fought the hijackers. About 3,000 people died in the attacks. Al-Qaeda, the terrorist group led by Saudi Arabian millionaire Osama bin Laden, claimed responsibility for the attacks. The world's attention focused on Afghanistan, where the Taliban were sheltering bin Laden. The Taliban refused to hand bin Laden over to the U.S. authorities or reveal where he was hiding. A U.S.-led coalition of forces invaded the country, saying they wanted to root out the terrorists and their supporters. The Taliban were driven out of power in Afghanistan, but neither its leader, Mullah Mohammed Omar, nor Osama bin Laden were found. More than 3,000 civilians are estimated to have been killed in the fighting.

In 2001, a conference in Bonn, Germany, established a process for political rebuilding of the country, and Hamid Karzai was made interim president. In 2004, Karzai became the first democratically elected president of Afghanistan. Elections for seats in the new government's legislative body, the National Assembly, were held in September 2005.

Focus on: Osama bin Laden

Osama bin Laden (1957 –) first became linked with Afghanistan as one of the mujahideen who fought against the Soviet Union in the 1970s, when it occupied the country. He supported the Taliban and shared their goal of creating an Islamic state in Afghanistan. In return, the Taliban allowed bin Laden to fund terrorist training camps in the country and hid him when he was charged with international terrorism. Osama bin Laden is thought to be the founder of Al-Qaeda, the Islamist organization that has carried out many terrorist attacks, including the September 11, 2001, attacks on the United States. He remains in hiding in spite of many attempts to find him.

 Did You Know?

The name "Taliban" comes from the Persian and Pashtun word *talib*, or religious student.

CHAPTER 3

Landscape and Climate

Afghanistan is shaped like a clenched fist with the thumb stuck out to the northeast. It covers an area of about 250,000 square miles (about 647,500 square kilometers), about the size of the state of Texas. Its maximum length from west to east is about 770 miles (1,240 kilometers); from north to south it is about 630 miles (1,015 km). It borders China, Iran, Pakistan, Tajikistan, Turkmenistan, and Uzbekistan, but it has no access to the sea. It is dominated by its mountains, which take up about half the country and divide it into three regions: the Central Highlands, the Northern Plains, and the Southwestern Plateau.

▲ A bright sun shines over the snowcapped mountains of the Hindu Kush. Afghanistan's mountains make it difficult to travel the country.

 Did You Know?

At 24,558 feet (7,485 m) above sea level, Noshaq (also called Nowshak) is the highest mountain in Afghanistan. It is also the second highest mountain of the Hindu Kush range (after Tirich Mir in Pakistan), which marks the border between Pakistan and Afghanistan. Noshaq was first climbed by a Japanese team in 1960.

A LAND OF EXTREMES

Most of Afghanistan has a subarctic mountain climate with dry, cold winters. In the Central Highlands, summer temperatures sometimes soar to about 120°F (49°C). The Northern Plains cover about 24,700 sq miles (64,000 sq km) of very fertile plains and hills. This is where most of the country's farming occurs and where minerals and natural gas have been found. The southwest of the country features high plateaus and sandy deserts (the Southwestern Plateau). The soil is mostly infertile and the climate dry and mild. In the western and southern regions, strong winds of up to 112 miles per hour (180 kilometers per hour) occur between June and September. These winds are known as the Winds of 120 Days. They can bring sand or dust storms.

Did You Know?

Afghanistan's mountains have many glaciers and year-round snow. The extremely cold weather in these areas makes it impossible to go to school. On many days, people cannot go out at all because it is too cold, and the snow is too deep. Midwinter temperatures as low as 16°F (-9°C) are common above 6,562 feet (2,000 m).

▼ These climbers on Mount Noshaq are approaching the summit of the mountain (25,558 feet/7,485 m). The summit can be seen in the distance.

Most of Afghanistan's precipitation falls between the months of October and April. The amount of precipitation varies by region: the deserts get less than 4 inches (100 millimeters) of rain a year, but the mountains receive more than 40 inches (1,000 mm), mostly as snow.

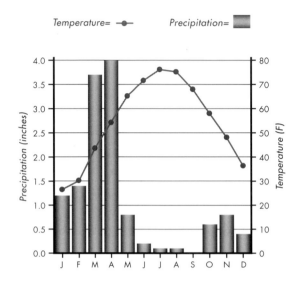

Temperature= ●   Precipitation= ▬

▲ Average monthly climate conditions in Kabul

RIVERS AND LAKES

Mountain streams feed many of Afghanistan's major rivers. The Amu Darya is the only river in the country on which boats can sail. The Hari Rud River forms part of the border with Iran, and the Helmand River is used extensively for irrigation and agriculture. The Kabul River flows east into Pakistan to join the Indus River, which empties into the Indian Ocean. Afghanistan has a few small lakes, including Zarkol, Shiveh, and the saline Lake Istadeh-ye Moqor.

EARTHQUAKES

Earthquakes are common in Afghanistan, and more than 1,300 have been recorded since A.D. 734. The country has so many earthquakes

▼ A boy hurries across a swaying bridge over the Kabul River near Sarobi. Many people live alongside Afghanistan's rivers, where the land is more fertile than on the dry plains.

because it lies on the southern fringe of the Eurasian tectonic plate, which collides with the Arabian plate, to the south, and the Indian plate, to the southeast. Major earthquakes occurred in 1998, 2002, 2004, and 2005.

▼ A girl screams as she is held by her father during the powerful aftershock from an earthquake in Nahrin, in the Hindu Kush. More than 2,000 people were killed and 30,000 were made homeless by the earthquake that struck in March 2002.

Focus on: Mountain Passes

Mountain passes, some of them extremely narrow, have been vital entry and exit points for those trying to conquer Afghanistan. Alexander the Great invaded the country through the Kushan Pass, in the west, and left it through the Khyber Pass, in the east, to invade India. The Moghul emperor Babur used the same passes to conquer both Afghanistan and India in the 1500s. During the Afghan wars in the nineteenth and twentieth centuries, many battles were fought in the Khyber Pass. The most famous of these battles took place in January 1842; 16,000 British and Indian troops were killed. The British constructed a road through the pass in 1879. A railroad was also built there in the 1920s. The Salang Pass, with its Soviet-built tunnel, was one of the main routes the Soviets used to invade Afghanistan in 1979.

CHAPTER 4

Population and Settlements

In 2005, Afghanistan's population was just over 31 million. Most of the country's people live in its countryside, and 44.6 percent of the population is under the age of 14. One reason for Afghanistan's young population is that its people do not live long; the harsh climate, poverty, and war mean that average life expectancy is just 43 years. Afghanistan has one of the lowest life expectancies in the world.

ETHNIC GROUPS

Afghanistan has four main ethnic groups and many smaller ones. The Pashtuns, or Pushtuns, are the largest group, making up 42 percent of the population. They are followed by the Tajiks (27 percent) and the Hazaras and the Uzbeks (9 percent each). Smaller groups include the Aimak, Turkmen, and Baluchi. The different groups are related to many of the ethnic groups of Iran, Pakistan, Tajikistan, Turkmenistan, and Uzbekistan. Many Pashtuns, for example, also live in northwestern Pakistan, where they are called Pathans.

In Afghanistan, these ethnic or tribal groupings define who a person is and are, therefore, very important. Historically, there has been rivalry and fighting between the different groups—and sometimes within them. Traditionally, the Pashtuns have been the dominant group. They speak Pashto, which is one of the two official languages of Afghanistan. They have a tribal code called *pashtunwali,* which emphasizes courage, honor, and hospitality. Hamid Karzai, who was elected president of Afghanistan in 2004, is a Pashtun. The Kuchi are a group of Pashtun who are nomads.

◀ A Hazara man repairs shoes on a street corner in Mazar-e Sharif. The Hazaras are generally not treated well by the other ethnic groups in Afghanistan.

The Tajiks speak Dari, or Afghan Persian, the other official language of Afghanistan. They are closely related to the people of Tajikistan and live in the valleys north of Kabul and in the region of Badakhshan. The Hazaras live in the center and the north of the country. Many Hazaras speak a dialect of the Persian language, with some Mongolian and Turkish vocabulary, but those in the major cities speak Dari.

The Hazaras have been discriminated against by the other groups and by successive governments, partly because they look different from other Afghans. The Uzbeks are the largest of a number of groups who speak Turkic languages. They live to the north of the Hindu Kush, near the Amu Darya River.

▼ In 1996, a group of Northern Alliance fighters walk along a road near Bagram. The Northern Alliance was mainly made up of Tajiks and Uzbeks who united to fight the Taliban.

 Did You Know?

The Asian appearance of the Hazaras means that many people think they are descended from the Mongols. Others say their ancestors came from the Xinjiang region of China. The Hazaras themselves believe that their ancestors were the original inhabitants of the region, the Buddhists who built the Bamiyan Buddhas.

Population Data

- Population: 31,056,997
- Population 0–14 yrs: 44.6%
- Population 15–64 yrs: 53%
- Population 65+ yrs: 2.4%
- Population growth rate: 2.67%
- Population density: 119.6 per sq mile/ 46.2 per sq km
- Urban population: 23%
- Major cities: Kabul 3,000,000

Source: CIA

▲ Most Afghan people live in rural areas like this farmland region in Jabul-Saraj. Mud-brick houses can be seen among the terraced fields of crops.

THE FAMILY AND THE VILLAGE

Seventy-six percent of people in Afghanistan live in villages. Families in the country are ruled by the male head of the household, and several generations may live together in a mud-brick house or compound (small settlement of houses). Most villages in Afghanistan have fewer than one hundred houses. The basic unit of social organization is known as the *qawm*, a grouping based on kinship and on where people live, but not necessarily on their ethnic group. Each village has three sources of authority: the *malik* (village headman), the *mirab* (master of water distribution), and the *mullah* (religious leader or teacher). Often a *khan*—the term means "large landowner" and can also mean "king"— takes on the role of both *malik* and *mirab*. These roles are always occupied by men.

TOWNS AND CITIES

Only about one quarter of Afghanistan's population lives in the cities, although it is predicted that half the population will be living in cities by 2015. The country's only major

urban region is Kabul, the capital, which has a
population of about three million people. Kabul
was founded over 3,000 years ago. Other major
cities include Herat, Jalalabad, Mazar-e Sharif,
and Kandahar. Many ancient structures in Kabul,
Herat, and Kandahar were reduced to rubble
during the wars, as were many new buildings.
Unemployment and the high cost of housing
have made life difficult for many city dwellers.

Focus on: Kabul

People from all over Afghanistan live in Kabul,
the country's largest city. It is situated in the
mountains, about 1,800 meters (5,900 ft) above
sea level, in a valley along the Kabul River.
The area around Kabul has one of the highest
densities of landmines in the world and has
suffered badly from the many years of war.

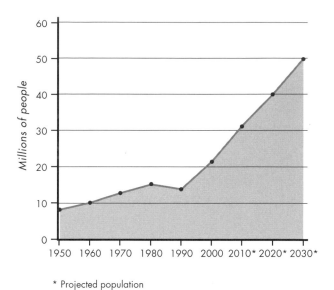

* Projected population

▲ Population growth, 1950-2030

▼ People returning to Kabul after years of war and
instability are building new homes on the outskirts of
the city.

CHAPTER 5

Government and Politics

Afghanistan is led by President Hamid Karzai, who was elected in October 2004 in the first presidential election to take place in the country since 1969. A Pashtun who also speaks several Afghan languages, Karzai had already been chosen as interim president by the U.S. government in 2002. In 2004, more than ten million Afghans registered to vote. Many potential candidates refused to stand, claiming that the elections were fraudulent. An independent commission did find evidence of fraud but said that it had not affected the results. Karzai won 55.4 percent of the vote. His cabinet includes members of the Northern Alliance, who fought alongside the United States in 2001. It also includes other representatives from Afghanistan's Loya Jirga, or Grand Council.

THE CONSTITUTION

In 2004, Afghanistan's new constitution established the country as an Islamic republic where men and women have equal rights and duties before the law. The United States held the power of veto (could make the final decision) over the document. Under the constitution, the government of Afghanistan has a president, two vice presidents, a Lower House (the Wolesi Jirga, which means "House of the People"), an Upper House (the Meshrano Jirga, which means "House of the

▼ Hamid Karzai (left), who was elected president of Afghanistan in 2004, speaks to the media while U.S. president George W. Bush listens at the White House, in Washington, D.C., in January 2002.

Elders"), and an independent legal system. Mohammed Zahir Shah, the country's former king, returned to the country in 2002 but does not have any power.

PARLIAMENT

The Wolesi Jirga that was elected in September 2005 includes former Taliban members, warlords, and mujahideen. The country has 68 women among a total of 249 members of parliament (MPs). The population of each of Afghanistan's 32 provinces elects MPs to serve five-year terms. At least two women must be elected from each province.

The Meshrano Jirga consists of 102 members. One-third of its members are voted in by provincial councils for four-year terms; one-third are elected by the district councils of each province for three-year terms; the final third is appointed by the president for five years. Half of the Meshrano Jirga must consist of women.

Focus on: The Loya Jirga

"Loya Jirga" is a Pashtun term meaning "Grand Council." It is a traditional gathering of elders from the different groups in Afghanistan, who come together to settle disputes. It dates back many centuries and is similar to the Muslim *shura,* or consultative assembly. The most famous Loya Jirga took place in Kandahar in 1747, when Pashtun tribal chiefs met to elect a king. After nine days, they still could not agree. The story goes that they chose the only man who had not spoken a word. His name was Ahmad Shah Durrani, and he went on to establish Afghanistan as a nation. The 2002 Loya Jirga included 2,000 delegates, 1,051 elected members, 100 seats for Afghan refugees, 6 seats for internally displaced Afghans, and 25 seats for nomads. For the first time, 160 seats were reserved for women. The 2003 Loya Jirga, which took until 2004 to establish the new constitution, was nicknamed the "loya jagra," or "big fight," because there were so many disputes.

▶ People gather at a meeting in Mazar-e Sharif in December 2003 to elect members of the Loya Jirga.

THE LEGAL SYSTEM

The legal system set up under Afghanistan's new constitution consists of the Stera Mahkama (Supreme Court), appeals courts, and lower district courts. Nine judges appointed by the president (and with the approval of the Wolesi Jirga) make up the Stera Mahkama, which has a ten-year term. Judges must be at least 40 years old. They must not belong to a political party, and they must have a degree in law or Islamic jurisprudence. One of them is appointed chief justice. A separate Afghan Independent Human Rights Commission investigates human rights abuses and war crimes.

The Stera Mahkama is the country's ultimate legal body. It has very conservative religious views. For example, in October 2005, Ali Mohaqiq Nasab, the male editor of a women's rights magazine, *Haqooq-i-Zan*, was jailed for two years after being convicted of blasphemy for publishing "anti-Islamic articles." These articles included a piece that challenged the belief that Muslims who convert to other religions should be stoned to death. The Stera Mahkama has also banned women from singing on television and called for an end to cable television in the country.

SECURITY

Security remains an important issue in the country. The government does not have power in many parts of the country, which are still controlled by warlords in charge of a total of about 50,000 armed militiamen. Afghanistan's national army, in contrast, has 14,000 troops. The International Security Assistance Force

▼ Ali Mohaqiq Nasab (second from right) is arrested on charges of blasphemy. On December 21, 2005, the Kabul High Court allowed Nasab to be released from jail after reducing his two-year sentence to six months.

 ► New women graduates of the National Police Training Centre stand to attention during a ceremony in Kandahar in June 2006. Under the Taliban, these women would not have been allowed to work outside the home.

(ISAF) currently numbers about 9,200 troops from 35 NATO and non-NATO countries. ISAF was created in December 2001 after the removal of the Taliban and has been controlled by NATO since 2003. Other foreign troops remain in the country to search for members of the Taliban and Al-Qaeda. There are also 19,000 U.S. soldiers, who were joined in the spring of 2006 by an additional 3,600 British troops. They are charged with the difficult task of rooting out the opium trade and have also been involved in fierce fighting against Taliban militias. In spite of the presence of these troops, violence in Afghanistan has escalated. At least 1,400 people in Afghanistan died in battles in 2005—the highest number since 2001.

Focus on: Women in Politics

Many conservative people in Afghanistan oppose women taking part in politics. Only a brave woman chooses to become an MP in a country where many women and girls are still afraid to leave home without the all-covering burqa because they face violence and harassment on the streets. Many men in the country think women should stay at home. When two female parliamentarians traveled with a delegation to London, England, without their husbands, some of the other male delegates said this should have been forbidden.

 Did You Know?

In Afghanistan's new political system, women make up 25 percent of the country's members of parliament, one of the highest proportions in the world. An index measuring inequality between men and women, however, puts Afghanistan above only one country in the world—Niger. It is debatable how much power Afghanistan's women actually have.

CHAPTER 6

Energy and Resources

Afghanistan is rich in resources, including natural gas, petroleum, coal, copper, chromite, talc, barite, sulphur, lead, zinc, iron ore, salt, and precious and semiprecious stones. The country's mountains, its history of conflict, and its lack of transportation make these resources difficult to exploit.

GEMSTONES

The northeastern regions of Afghanistan are some of the most important gem-producing areas of the world. The Hindu Kush is the western end of a gem-producing region that stretches along the Himalayas. Lapis lazuli; emeralds from the Panjshir Valley; green, blue, and pink tourmaline; kunzite; and some rubies from the area between Jalalabad and Kabul have been found. But these treasures are difficult to extract and transport. Rough-cut Panjshir emeralds, for example, must be taken on foot to northern Pakistan, a journey of about 124 miles (200 km) that can take up to 20 days through mountains booby-trapped with landmines. The emeralds are then bought by Pakistani or Western buyers and taken away to be cut and sold.

COAL, OIL, AND NATURAL GAS

The region around the Caspian Sea, to the north of Afghanistan, has more oil and natural gas than either the United States or the North Sea. It is worth about U.S.$5 trillion at today's prices. Gas reserves in Turkmenistan are estimated to be the fifth largest in the world,

▼ The man holding an emerald in his fingers checks the gemstone's purity at an auction near Bazarak in 1999.

and Kazakhstan is expected to become one of the world's largest oil producers. Afghanistan is not yet producing oil, although some people say that it has similar huge potential.

Natural gas was discovered in Afghanistan in 1967. After the Soviet invasion in 1979, most of the country's gas was directed to the Soviet Union's natural gas grid using a link through Uzbekistan. In the 1980s, natural gas accounted for 56 percent of Afghanistan's export revenues. After the Soviets left, the country's natural gas fields were capped. Its latest figure for gas production is about 7.8 billion cubic feet

 Did You Know?

Almost half of Afghanistan's energy comes from firewood.

▶ Workers load coal onto a mule before taking it to Kabul. Afghanistan's years of war have badly disrupted the country's energy supplies.

(220 million cubic meters), although estimates say it has reserves of about 1.8 trillion cubic feet (50 billion cubic meters) of natural gas.

Focus on: The Koh-i-Noor Diamond

The Koh-i-Noor (Mountain of Light) diamond is said to be 5,000 years old and was originally supposed to have weighed 793 carats. Hindus claim that it was stolen from their god, Krishna. It was acquired by the Moghuls in 1526. The story goes that, in 1739, the Moghul emperor Mohammed Shah kept it hidden in his turban. The Persian king, Nadir Shah, engineered a public trading of turbans that the emperor could not refuse. Through this trade, Nadir Shah acquired the jewel. When Nadir Shah was assassinated in 1747, General Ahmad Shah Abdali took the diamond to Kabul and passed it to his son and his grandson, Shah Shuja, who became king. When Shah Shuja was deposed in 1813, he is believed to have given the diamond to Maharajah Ranjit Singh, the governor of Lahore, who freed him from prison. The diamond was lost until 1849, when the British found it in the treasury in Lahore, Pakistan, and it was presented to Queen Victoria. She had it recut, reducing its weight from 186 carats to 108.93 carats, and it became part of the British Crown Jewels. Many groups from Afghanistan, including the Taliban, have tried to reclaim the diamond, but it remains in Britain.

▲ A woman and her child at home in Kabul in 2005. They have a fan and a radio, but they have to use a lantern for lighting because the electricity supply is often interrupted. Many ordinary people in Afghanistan have this problem.

Afghanistan is estimated to have 65.2 million tons (66.2 metric tons) of coal reserves, most of which are in the north of the country. Coal has been discovered in the Hindu Kush; in Karkar and Eshposhteh, in Baghlan province; and in Balkh province. The country produced more than 89,285 tons (90,719 metric tons) of coal a year in the early 1990s, but by 2002, the country was producing only about 893 tons (907 metric tons).

ELECTRICITY

Afghanistan has considerable potential for hydroelectric power. The country has dams and hydroelectric stations on the Kondoz, Kabul,

Arghandab, and Helmand Rivers. Before and during the Taliban years and during the U.S.-led invasion in 2001, however, transmission lines were brought down and turbines and floodgates

Energy Data

- Energy consumption as % of world total: not available

- Energy consumption by sector (% of total)
  Industry: not available
  Transportation: not available
  Agriculture: not available
  Services: not available
  Residential: not available
  Other: not available

- CO_2 emissions as % of world total: 0.004

- CO_2 emissions per capita in tons per year: 0

Source: World Resources Institute

were blown up. As a result, hydroelectric power production almost stopped. It is now starting up again. In January 2003, the Northwest Kabul Thermal Power Station was recommissioned after lying inactive for 14 years. This alone has almost doubled the available power supply in Kabul, which is particularly important during the winter months, when demand increases by one-third. In addition, several diesel generators have been installed in smaller provincial cities throughout the country that had little or no access to electricity, including Faizabad, Baghdis, Bamiyan, Samanghan, and Uruzgan. Some electricity is imported from neighboring countries. The cities of Herat, Mazar-e Sharif, and Kunduz have forged agreements with neighboring Iran, Uzbekistan, and Tajikistan to import energy.

Less than 10 percent of Afghanistan's people have access to electricity. Ismail Khan, a former warlord who is now Afghanistan's energy minister, says that Kabul will not have full power until 2008.

Focus on: Pipelines

Many countries have had their eye on the oil under the Caspian Sea for some time. Russian and German companies wanted to build a pipeline through Eastern Europe, but this plan was abandoned when the former Yugoslavia was bombed during the 1990s. Russia and China have also negotiated with Iran and Kazakhstan about constructing a pipeline. In 1998, a consortium led by Unocal, an American oil company, started negotiations with the Taliban about a pipeline through Afghanistan, but the talks failed. In 2002, Afghanistan's government signed an agreement with Pakistan and Turkmenistan to take gas from Turkmenistan through Afghanistan to India and Pakistan. Villages along the route would be supplied with gas, Afghanistan's government would be paid for the gas passing through the country, and Afghanistan would own the pipeline after 30 years.

► This section of pipeline near Mazar-e Sharif is part of a line that carries gas from Turkmenistan through Afghanistan and, finally, to India and Pakistan.

CHAPTER 7

Economy and Income

Afghanistan is an extremely poor country. Eighty percent of its people are farmers, many of whom only grow enough food for themselves and their families. Two-thirds of the country's people live on less than U.S.$2 a day, and more than half of the population lives below the poverty line. The legacy of war and continuing conflict makes it difficult for things to improve. In 2004, Afghanistan still ranked the lowest of all 177 countries listed in the Human Development Index by the United Nations Development Program.

Economically, Afghanistan is still very dependent on foreign aid, which amounts to 3.4 times the national revenue and accounts for 46 percent of the country's Gross Domestic Product (GDP). According to the World Bank, Afghanistan's operating budget for 2005 was U.S.$600 million. Half of this came from taxes and the other half from international donors. It is estimated that Afghans living outside the country invested U.S.$3 billion in the country (out of an economy with a GDP of about U.S.$6–$7 billion).

PRODUCE, IMPORTS, AND EXPORTS

Afghanistan produces wheat, fruits, nuts, wool, mutton, sheepskins, lambskins, soap, furniture, shoes, fertilizer, cement, textiles, and hand-woven carpets. Karakul sheep are raised in large numbers in the north. The tight, curly fleece of Karakul lambs is used to make Persian lamb coats. The country also produces the sweet grapes and melons that are grown mostly in the west, in the area north of the Hindu Kush, and in the fertile regions around Herat.

◄ A man with oxen plows a field on his family farm in May 2006. Many Afghans are farmers.

Focus on: Carpets

Afghan rugs and carpets are famous throughout the world. Those made by Turkmen and some Uzbeks are usually dark red with geometrical figures. The Baluchi make prayer rugs. Afghan carpets are made of wool, camel hair, or cotton.

▼ This picture shows women in the village of Boi Temur weaving a rug in April 2006. Rug-weaving is one way in which women can earn money for themselves and their families.

Did You Know?

In September 2002, Afghanistan replaced its "Old Afghani" notes with "New Afghani" notes that were worth 100 times as much as the old ones. The old currency had been devalued so many times it had become almost worthless. Some Afghan people use U.S. dollars and currencies from neighboring countries because they believe they can rely on other, more stable currencies not to lose their value.

Economic Data

- Gross National Income (GNI) in U.S.$: 5,543,000,000
- World rank by GNI: 120
- GNI per capita in U.S.$: less than 825
- World rank by GNI per capita: not specified but estimated to be below 210th
- Economic growth: 8.0%

Source: World Bank

In 1975, Afghanistan was self-sufficient in wheat, and grain was its main export. However, between 1998 and 2001, years of first, drought, and then, war, resulted in poor or nonexistent harvests. Today, Afghanistan only produces enough to feed half its population, and it imports eight times more goods than it exports.

SMUGGLING

For many years, governments of Afghanistan have profited from the trade in illegal goods across the country's borders. Televisions, cigarettes, guns, and drugs all passed through Afghanistan on their way to Pakistan or Iran. In this way, the traders avoided paying the high taxes imposed by other countries, and the government of Afghanistan received a share of the profits. A United Nations study estimated that, in 2000, "unofficial" exports from Afghanistan to Pakistan and Iran were worth U.S.$941 million and U.S.$139 million, respectively. The Taliban was said to have made between U.S.$36 million and U.S.$75 million in this way, in spite of the fact that it placed an official ban on consumer goods in Afghanistan.

OPIUM

Today, Afghanistan's main trade is in opium, and the country is the world's largest producer of this drug. The red opium poppy was supposedly introduced to Afghanistan by Alexander the Great (356–323 B.C.). Opium

▼ Under the Taliban, TVs, radios, and computers were not allowed to be brought into Afghanistan from other countries. Some people made their own consumer goods, like these satellite dishes in a Kabul market, and smuggling was widespread.

▲ A farmer watches as his illegal poppy crop in Kandahar is destroyed by officials using a tractor and plow. Authorities are working to stamp out poppy production. Many farmers grow the illegal crop because they can make more money from it than from growing anything else.

comes from the plant's unripe seed heads. It can be made quickly, and it is easy to transport. It offers an important source of income, especially to poor farmers. These farmer can make about U.S.$5,200 from an acre of opium but only U.S.$121 from an acre of wheat. Recent efforts to stamp out opium growing in Afghanistan have not been successful, partly because the money from the opium trade is crucial not only to the farmers but also to maintaining the power of the warlords and to the country itself. The International Monetary Fund (IMF) estimates that between 40 and 60 percent of Afghanistan's GDP comes from trade in opium. Between 80 and 90 percent of Europe's heroin,

an illegal drug, comes from Afghan poppies. Between 2001 and 2005, the number of provinces producing opium increased from just six to 28 (out of a total of 32 provinces). During that time, the export value of Afghanistan's opium was U.S.$2.3 billion. Afghanistan's opium harvest was predicted to increase by nearly 60 percent in 2006.

 Did You Know?

Afghanistan's central bank was founded in 1938. It issues money, lends money to cities and other banks, and is in charge of government loans.

CHAPTER 8

Global Connections

Despite its difficult terrain, Afghanistan has always had connections with other parts of the world. Its people have seen conquerors come and go, and they have traded with the many countries on their borders. Afghanistan was crossed by the famous Silk Route, an 5,000-mile (8,000-km) network of interconnecting roads which, between 500 B.C. and A.D. 1500, was the main route between Europe, the Near East, India, and China. During this time, exotic and commercial goods, skills, knowledge, and religion—as well explorers such as Marco Polo—crisscrossed the European and Asian continents and helped to shape the course of their history and culture.

REFUGEES

The conflict of the past 27 years has seen thousands of Afghan people fleeing abroad, mostly to Iran and Pakistan but also to the West. Afghans make up one of the largest groups of refugees and internally displaced people in the world. Since 2001, the United Nations has been able to bring back to Afghanistan more than 3.5 million people, mainly from Pakistan and Iran. Some of these people are playing an important role in the reconstruction of their country. But many Afghan refugees do not feel safe to return, and more than two million of them remain abroad. In addition to Afghan refugees abroad, between 167,000 and 200,000 people are displaced in the south and west of Afghanistan itself.

▼ People wait at the Chaman border crossing into Pakistan in November 2001. Pakistan closed its border with Afghanistan to deter the number of refugees fleeing the country because of war.

▲ Men rebuild homes on the Shomali Plain outside Kabul. Many homes in Afghanistan are being rebuilt after decades of war.

FORGING LINKS

More than 20 years of war have left Afghanistan not only poor but also cut off from the rest of the world. Rebuilding its transportation and communications systems is crucial to the country's reconstruction. Rebuilding its links with other countries, including its trading links, is also very important. International aid is still a major part of the country's income. In 2004, Afghanistan's main export partners were Pakistan, India, the United States, and Germany. Its main import partners were

 Did You Know?

Guyana, in South America, has a sizeable Afghan community. Afghans first arrived in Guyana more than 150 years ago.

Pakistan, the United States, India, Germany, Turkmenistan, Kenya, South Korea, and Russia. Some of these countries, such as Germany and Kenya, have many Afghan refugees.

Focus on: The Land of the Afghans

The various peoples who have come from different countries to rule Afghanistan over the years have given it many different names. One theory says that the name "Afghanistan" comes from combining the alternative name for the Pashtun rulers, the *Afghans*, and the Persian word *stan*, meaning country or land. Another theory is that the word came from an ancient people known as *Ashvakas*, or the horse people. One of the first names for the area was *Ariana*, the Greek version of the ancient *Aryanam Vaeja,* or Land of the Aryans. The first Persian conquerors called the region the Province of Khorasan.

In 2004, Afghanistan's exports were worth U.S.$446 million, while its imports amounted to about U.S.$3.7 billion. Its main exports—in addition to illegal opium—are fruits, nuts, hand-woven carpets, wool, cotton, hides and pelts, and precious and semiprecious gems. Its imports include machinery, tools, food, textiles, and petroleum products.

REGIONAL COOPERATION

In December 2005, Afghanistan hosted a regional conference on economic cooperation that involved 12 countries, including the six that share borders with Afghanistan, plus India, Turkey, the United Arab Emirates, Kazakhstan, and Kyrgyzstan. The conference aimed to promote economic cooperation in areas including electricity and energy generation, transportation, trade, border management, and investment.

The country's years of conflict have left the people of Afghanistan in need of training to update their skills. A number of projects—for example, the Kabul Distance Learning Center—have been set up to train teachers, midwives, journalists, and civil servants, as well as to link people via the Internet and e-mail. The World Bank has set up a project that aims to improve performance at ten of the country's universities through partnership programs with universities in other countries.

Did You Know?

Abdul Ahad Mohmand was the first Afghan cosmonaut (the Soviet term for astronaut). Before he became a cosmonaut, Mohmand served in the Afghan Air Force. In 1988, he spent nine days in space aboard the Russian Mir space station.

Focus on: Al-Qaeda and its Training Camps

Since the Soviet invasion of Afghanistan, young Muslim men have been taught how to fight using guerrilla tactics at military training camps in the country. Under the Taliban, military camps in Afghanistan, some of them run by Al-Qaeda, attracted an estimated 70,000 young Muslims from around the world. In these camps, the men were given basic training for several weeks or months in the use of weapons and explosives. They were also taught the Taliban's and Al-Qaeda's brand of anti-Western Islamic philosophy.

▶ A man who used to be a Taliban fighter shows a leaflet offering a reward for information to help with the capture of Al-Qaeda leaders Ayman al-Zawahiri (pictured on the left of the leaflet) and Osama bin Laden (right).

Focus on: The Kabul Distance Learning Center

In November 2002, a distance learning center supported by the World Bank was established in Kabul. It is now used to assist with the sharing of development knowledge between people in Afghanistan and their counterparts around the world. The Kabul Distance Learning Center makes use of information and communications technologies. The center's first video conference connected experts in Tajikistan, Kazakhstan, Uzbekistan, and the United States to discuss development prospects in Afghanistan. Through the center, Afghanistan's government agencies have been connected to the Internet, giving them access to e-mail for the first time.

► Women learn computer skills at an education center in Kabul. Information technology is opening up new opportunities for international cooperation and helps people keep informed about the world around them.

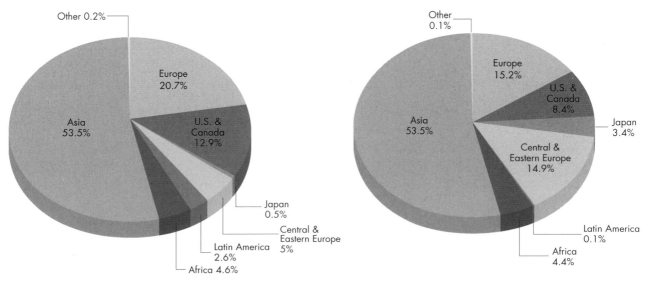

Destination of exports by major trading region

- Other 0.2%
- Europe 20.7%
- Asia 53.5%
- U.S. & Canada 12.9%
- Japan 0.5%
- Central & Eastern Europe 5%
- Latin America 2.6%
- Africa 4.6%

Origin of imports by major trading region

- Other 0.1%
- Europe 15.2%
- U.S. & Canada 8.4%
- Japan 3.4%
- Asia 53.5%
- Central & Eastern Europe 14.9%
- Latin America 0.1%
- Africa 4.4%

CHAPTER 9

Transportation and Communications

Traveling in Afghanistan is not easy. Most transportation for ordinary people is either on foot or by donkey. Many nomadic people in the country trek many miles by foot every day. In winter, the weather makes it impossible to travel or reach many parts of the country. Some of the country's roads have recently been repaired, but many are not in usable condition.

Although they existed in the past, there are no railways in Afghanistan today, other than a few miles of track across a bridge from Uzbekistan.

▼ In Kabul, two men pull a cart loaded with firewood. The ruined Darulaman Palace can be seen in the background.

Transport & Communications Data

- Total roads: 21,618 miles/34,789 km
- Total paved roads: 5,115 miles/8,231 km
- Total unpaved roads: 16,503 miles/ 26,558 km
- Total railways: n/a
- Major airports: 10
- Cars per 1,000 people: 9.4
- Cellular phones per 1,000 people: 21
- Personal computers per 1,000 people: n/a
- Internet users per 1,000 people: 0.9

Source: World Bank and CIA World Factbook

Focus on: The Salang Tunnel

Built at an altitude of 11,155 feet (3,400 m), the 1.7-mile (2.7-km) Salang Tunnel is one of the highest tunnels in the world. It connects the north and south of Afghanistan and also links the country with Uzbekistan and Tajikistan. When the tunnel is open, it takes ten hours to travel from Kabul to the north of the country; when it is closed, the journey takes 72 hours. The Salang Tunnel was built by the Soviets in 1964.

During fighting in 1998, the tunnel's southern entrance and its ventilation system were destroyed. In July 2004, the tunnel opened for the first time since 1997. By this time, ventilation shafts had been reconstructed, and tunnel lighting, ventilation equipment, and electric power generators had been installed. Since 2001, the tunnel has become a crucial link in the rebuilding of Afghanistan as a whole.

◀ A bus leaves the rebuilt Salang Tunnel that was reopened in 2004. The tunnel helps to connect Kabul with Mazar-e Sharif.

Barges loaded with goods navigate the Amu Darya River, which forms part of Afghanistan's border with Turkmenistan, Uzbekistan, and Tajikistan. During their occupation of the country, the Soviets completed a bridge across the Amu Darya and built the motor vehicle and railway bridge between Termez, in Uzbekistan, and Jeyretan, in Afghanistan.

REBUILDING THE SYSTEM

An efficient transportation system in Afghanistan is essential for the delivery of aid to the people of the country who need it and the rebuilding of the country's infrastructure—both of which are important for helping Afghanistan get back on its feet. Since 2001, reconstruction projects have focused on rebuilding roads and improving transportation. In January 2005, a major road linking Afghanistan with Iran was opened. Other road projects include a 242-mile (389-km) highway linking Kabul with Kandahar that was opened in 2004. In addition, about 603 miles (970 km) of rural roads are being improved.

THE MEDIA

Afghanistan's first newspaper was printed in 1875. Under Amanullah Shah, the country's media flourished, but it was not a free press. In the 1950s, the government controlled 95 percent of Afghanistan's media. The country's first radio station was opened in 1925, but it was destroyed in 1929 during the uprising against Amanullah Shah. Broadcasting began again when Radio Kabul started transmitting in 1940.

After the 1978 coup, Afghanistan's press was suppressed. Afghans secretly printed *shabnamah*, or "night letters," that contained uncensored news and opinions. Most other papers written by Afghans with news about their country were published outside Afghanistan. In the early 1990s, the country had ten newspapers. Under the Taliban, the media was strictly controlled and carried only government and religious information. Radio Kabul (which had become Radio Afghanistan in 1960) was renamed "Radio Voice of Sharia," in line with the strict Islamic law, and television was banned.

In 2001, following the removal of the Taliban, the country's media revived. Radio Afghanistan was one of the earliest stations to restart, broadcasting the first music the country had heard in many years. Radio is Afghanistan's main medium, and 85 percent of the population has access to it. Today, many small privately run (as well as state run) radio stations broadcast regularly, and the country has at least ten television stations. Restrictions on the media are still in place, however, and criticism of Islam is forbidden. In April 2005, Taliban radio was heard in Kandahar once again, supposedly broadcast using mobile transmission facilities.

TELEPHONES

There are still very few landline telephones in Afghanistan. The country has one telephone line for every ten people and even fewer lines in rural areas. The number of cellular phones in the country is slowly growing. In 2003, two cellular phone companies started operating in

◀ A live interview is conducted on Aina, a women's radio station in Kabul. Aina is one of many small radio stations that have sprung up in Afghanistan now that the Taliban no longer controls the media.

Afghanistan. The country now has about 170,000 mobile phone users.

Five VSATs (satellite connections) have been installed—in Kabul, Herat, Mazar-e Sharif, Kandahar, and Jalalabad—providing international and domestic voice and data connections. Two private mobile phone companies have been licensed to operate. Like urban young people everywhere, the youth of Afghanistan are eager to get connected. While Internet access is limited, Kabul now has both Internet cafés and public "telekiosks," at which anyone can go online for a small fee.

? Did You Know?

Afghanistan set up its Internet domain name—www.af—in 2003. This is now the Afghanistan government Web site.

▲ The main market in Mazar-e Sharif has a big billboard advertising telecommunications service. Cellular phone use and Internet use has gradually increased in Afghanistan in recent years.

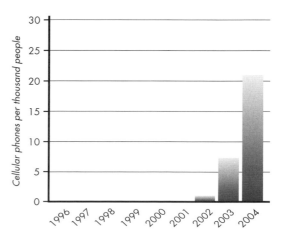

▲ Cellular phone use, 1996–2004

Education and Health

About one out of five Afghans is of school age. According to the World Bank, Afghanistan has the highest ratio of school-age children to adults in the world, and this reflects the young average age of the population. From the late 1950s until the Soviet invasion in 1979, education in Afghanistan was valued highly, and both boys and girls attended school and university. Kabul University had students from other parts of Asia and the Middle East. After the Soviet invasion, war made education difficult. Under the Taliban, boys generally received education in Islamic madrassas. Madrassas had always been an alternative to the school system; they focus on teaching Arabic and the Koran rather than basic skills. The Taliban forbade girls from going to school. As a result, Afghanistan's literacy rate, particularly among women, is one of the lowest in the world. Only 28 percent of people over the age of 15 (43 percent of men and 13 percent of women) can read, write, and do basic math. In 2004, only 36 percent of children went to primary school. In some provinces, over 61 percent of children were not enrolled. Nearly 80 percent of the country's 6,900 schools were damaged or destroyed in fighting during the Taliban years.

HIGHER EDUCATION

Under the Taliban, only a few students went on to higher education. Of these, all were male and most studied religious subjects. During this time, only four universities were open. By 2006, the country had 14, including those in Mazar-e Sharif, Herat, and Kandahar. Kabul has universities, polytechnics, and a medical school. Women are now allowed to attend but, because so many missed out on education during the Taliban years, very few are qualified for higher education.

◀ In 2002, a schoolgirl in Agha Ali village, in Kharaja, shows what she has learned. Although girls were not allowed to go to school when the Taliban was in power, some girls went to secret classes during this time.

THE SITUATION TODAY

In 2003, the Back to School campaign launched by Afghanistan's interim government led to an estimated three million children and 70,000 teachers returning to school. But more than 70 percent of schools still need repairs. Only half of the schools have clean water, and fewer than 40 percent have adequate sanitation. In 2006, Taliban rebels carried out 99 attacks on schools and made 37 threats against schools and communities. The United Nations Children's Fund (UNICEF) reported that six children had died as a result of the violence.

Education and Health Data

- Life expectancy at birth, male: 43.16
- Life expectancy at birth, female: 43.53
- Infant mortality rate per 1,000: 165
- Under-five mortality rate per 1,000: 257
- Physicians per 1,000 people: n/a
- Health expenditure as % of GDP: 7%
- Education expenditure as % of GDP: n/a
- Primary net enrollment: 54%
- Student-teacher ratio, primary school: 65
- Adult literacy as % age 15+: 28%

Source: United Nations Agencies and World Bank

Focus on: Education for Girls

Under the Taliban, girls were not allowed to go to school at all. Some attended illegal classes in one another's houses, at great risk to themselves and their teachers. In spite of campaigns to get girls back to school since the end of Taliban rule, UNICEF estimates that more than one million of Afghanistan's primary-school-age girls are still not enrolled. In five of the country's 32 provinces, 90 percent of primary-school-age girls do not attend school. Afghanistan's Ministry of Education and UNICEF have allocated U.S.$19 million to help establish community-based classes for up to 500,000 girls in villages and provide training programs for 25,000 primary-school teachers. The lack of qualified female teachers is another problem facing education for girls in the country.

◀ These women are taking an adult literacy class in Hesarak village in northern Afghanistan. Under the Taliban, girls were not allowed to go to school, so many women in the country have never learned to read and write.

 A woman in Afghanistan receives a check-up at a clinic for mothers and children. Many of the people seen at this clinic are being treated for the illnesses and injuries common in a war zone.

HEALTH

The health of Afghanistan's people is one of the worst in the world. Life expectancy, at only 43 years, is one of the lowest in the world; the average life expectancy for people living in low-income countries is 59. Afghanistan is at the bottom of the 177 countries listed in the United Nations 2004 Human Development Report.

The country's infant and maternal mortality rates are also among the highest in the world. One out of six children dies in infancy, and one woman dies from pregnancy-related causes about every 30 minutes. Diseases that are no longer a problem in other countries are still very serious in Afghanistan. Thirty percent of Afghanistan's children under five have diarrhea. More than 60 percent of all childhood deaths and disabilities in Afghanistan are the result of respiratory infections, diarrhea, and diseases preventable with vaccines, especially measles. Tuberculosis and malaria are common.

Did You Know?

The World Health Organization estimates that between 30 and 50 percent of the population of a country experiencing conflict such as that in Afghanistan will find that their mental health is affected. Mental health problems, however, are not being treated because of the upheaval caused by ongoing war and other pressing needs.

Part of the reason for Afghanistan's extremely poor national health is that only 13 percent of Afghans have access to safe water, only 12 percent have access to adequate water and sanitation, and only 6 to 10 percent have access to electricity. Sixty-five percent have no way of getting to a clinic or other health-care service. There is a high risk of injury by landmines, and many victims die before they can reach a place where they can be treated. The country also has a shortage health-care workers. The country especially needs female health-care workers, because most Afghan women want to be treated only by another woman.

WHAT IS BEING DONE?

In 2004, the U.S. government donated U.S.$83 million for improving health in Afghanistan. It was hoped that 830 new midwives could be trained at a new midwifery school in Kabul by the end of 2006. UNICEF has organized mass vaccination programs to immunize Afghan children against the most common diseases; polio is close to being eradicated altogether. But improving health in Afghanistan is a massive task. The whole health-care system needs to be constructed, and its most basic elements are still

not in place. Lack of security makes it difficult to reach the most needy areas. In 2004, the international humanitarian aid organization Médecins Sans Frontières (Doctors Without Borders) withdrew from Afghanistan after five of its staff were killed in an ambush.

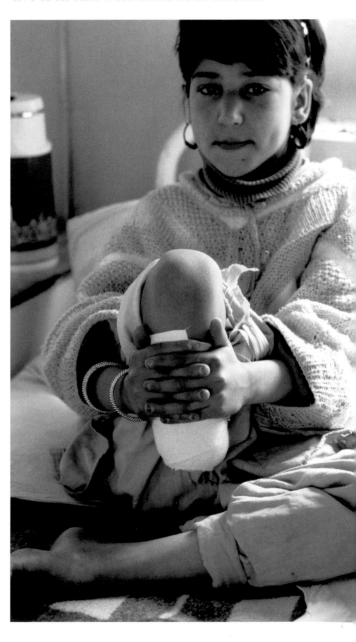

▲ This girl in a hospital in Kabul has had her foot amputated. Her injury was caused by stepping on one of the many landmines planted in Afghanistan.

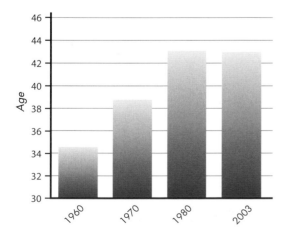

▲ Life expectancy at birth, 1960–2003

CHAPTER 11

Culture and Religion

For thousands of years, Afghanistan was a crossing point for conquerors and traders, and many of them left their treasures and part of their heritage behind. The country still has some beautiful ancient buildings, priceless artworks, and precious gemstones, though some of them were looted or destroyed during the years of conflict. Coins dating from the eighth century B.C. and from countries as far apart as India, Italy, Egypt, and Greece have been found in Afghanistan. The two beautiful mosques of Herat and Mazar-e Sharif are world famous. Other less well-known but equally remarkable sites include the 1,000-year-old Great Arch of Qal'eh-ye Bost; the Chel Zina, or the Forty Steps; rock inscriptions made by the Moghul emperor Babur, in Kandahar; the Towers of Victory, in Ghazni; Emperor Babur's tomb; and the great Bala Hissar fortress, in Kabul. Many ancient treasures were housed in the Kabul Museum, but the museum was bombed in 1993 and then looted by the Taliban. Items taken from the collection still turn up from time to time in different parts of the world.

Afghanistan has a long history of arts and crafts, and many of these are still practiced today. Herat, for example, is famous for its blue-green tiles, and craftsmen there also make gold and silver jewelry, embroidery, rugs, carpets, and leather goods.

▼ This beautiful mosque in Mazar-e Sharif is a shrine to Hazrat Ali, who was a cousin and son-in-law of the Prophet Mohammed.

Focus on: The Bamiyan Buddhas

The two enormous Buddhas of Bamiyan were thought to date back to the third century. They were 174 feet (53 m) and 118 feet (36 m) high and were the tallest standing Buddhas in the world. The Taliban blew them up in 2001 because they believe that all representations of human figures are anti-Islamic. There is now a plan by the Japanese artist Hiro Yamagata to create a laser projection of the original Buddhas on the site, using solar energy.

MUSIC

Afghans have always loved music. *Klasik* is Afghanistan's classical musical form. At least 14 different instruments are native to Afghanistan. They include the tabla, a pair of hand drums; a two-stringed instrument called the *damboura*; the *chang*, a plucked mouth harp; the lutelike *seta* and *sarang*; a type of flute called the *tula*; the *dilruba*, a bowed string instrument; and the *harmonya*, an accordion-style instrument. The *rabab*, or *rubab*, is another instrument that is like a lute and is considered by some to be the country's national instrument. The singer Ahmad Zahir is one of Afghanistan's best-loved popular musicians and his music can be listened to on the Internet. Ustad Mahwash is one of Afghanistan's best-known female singers and one of the few Afghan women to have trained with the classical masters. Safdar Tawakuli, a Hazara, is famous for playing the *damboura* and has been performing in Kabul now that the Taliban's ban on music has been lifted.

▲ Mirwais Najrabi (left), age 13, is accompanied on the Indian keyboard by his older brother, Nur-ul-Haq, in their Kabul home. Some young male musicians have become famous in Afghanistan. Since the fall of the Taliban, their songs are being heard once again in the country.

 Did You Know?

The Taliban banned music and dance. The group also banned television and punished anyone caught watching it.

 Did You Know?

The Minaret of Jam, in western Afghanistan, is the second-tallest brick tower in the world. The tallest is Qutub Minar, in New Delhi, India.

▶ This hairdressing salon in Kabul is doing good business now that Afghan women are allowed to go outdoors and dress fashionably again. The Taliban had placed severe restrictions on the country's women.

POETRY AND PHILOSOPHY

Afghanistan has always produced poets and philosophers. Afghan poetry often reflects the people's pride in their country. One of the country's most famous thinkers is Ibn-e-Sina-e-Balkhi, or Avicenna of Balkh, who was born in Balkh in A.D. 980 and was a famous philosopher and scientist. Another is Jelauddin Rumi, a poet and founder of the Mawlawi Sufi Order, a leading mystical brotherhood of Islam.

CLOTHING

In the country's villages, both men and women wear baggy cotton trousers. Men wear long cotton shirts, wide sashes around their waists, a skullcap, and sometimes a turban. Women wear a long, loose shirt or dress; a colorful, swirling skirt over their trousers; and a shawl wrapped around their heads. The clothes Afghan people wear also depends on their ethnic group. Hazara women, for example, wear colorful red and green embroidered dresses over full trousers. In the cities, clothing styles vary greatly, with some wearing traditional dress and others modern clothes.

 Did You Know?

For 800 years, Afghanistan had a small Jewish community. At its largest, this group numbered about 5,000 people. Today, only one Jew—Zablon Simintov—remains in the country.

 Did You Know?

The sacred cloak of the Prophet Mohammed is kept locked away in Kandahar. It is only displayed on very rare and special occasions. Mullah Omar, the leader of the Taliban, famously showed it to people in 1996. Until that time, it had not been taken out for 60 years.

RELIGION

In Afghanistan, over 98 percent of the people are Muslim. Of this group, 89.2 percent are Sunni and 8.9 per cent are Shi'ia. The majority of Hazaras are Shi'a. The remaining 1.9 percent of the country's population includes Hindu and Sikh minorities, some of whom returned after the removal of the Taliban.

The people of Afghanistan celebrate Muslim holidays such as Eid al-Fitr and Eid al-Adha in the same way as most Muslims in other countries. They attend their mosques, visit friends and family, and prepare special foods. These Muslim holidays are all based on the cycles of the moon, but other holidays celebrated in Afghanistan, such as Norooz, are based on the Sun's movement. Norooz is celebrated on March 21, the spring equinox, when the Sun appears for exactly 12 hours in the day. Jeshen, celebrated on August 19, is Afghan Independence Day. This holiday commemorates the day that British rule finally ended following the Third Afghan War.

◀ A balloon seller in Kabul waits for customers during the build-up to the Muslim festival of Eid al-Adha.

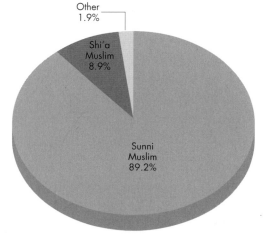

▲ Major religions

Other
1.9%

Shi'a
Muslim
8.9%

Sunni
Muslim
89.2%

 Did You Know?

The beautiful fifteenth-century Blue Mosque at Mazar-e Sharif is an important place of pilgrimage for Shi'a Muslims. It is believed to be the tomb of the Muslim leader Hazrat Ali, who was the cousin and son-in-law of the Prophet Mohammed. In 1220, it was covered in earth to protect it from Genghis Khan and was not rediscovered until the 1480s.

CHAPTER 12

Leisure and Tourism

Today, most Afghans have to eat what they can get, especially in the countryside. Many of Afghanistan's traditional foods, however, are delicious. Some dishes are similar to Persian, Asian, or Middle Eastern foods, but there are many that are only found in Afghanistan, such as fried leek pastries, called

boolawnee; Afghani lamb with spinach; *samoos-i-yirakot*, or stuffed vegetable turnovers; and Kabuli *pilau*, a dish of rice and chicken. The staple food is unleavened bread called nan. Nan is eaten with vegetables, fruit, rice, and sometimes meat. Most people in the country drink strong, black tea sweetened with a solid type of sugar that is like molasses.

Focus on: Nan Bread

Nan is a traditional type of flat, unleavened bread also found in other countries in the region. In the countryside, it is baked on hot stones. In the cities, bakeries have circular fire-pits with cement walls. People take their homemade dough to be baked here. The baker rolls it out, makes little holes in it to keep it thin, and puts it against the side of the fire-pit. The baker takes it out before it gets burned.

EXTREME SPORTS

The sport of *buzkashi* is unique to Afghanistan. *Buzkashi* means "goat killing." The game is played on horseback and dates back many centuries. Only male stud horses are used in the game and they are specially trained. *Buzkashi* horsemen wear thick hats, quilted coats, long boots, and strong scarves wound around their

▼ This shop sells nan bread, a staple of the Afghan diet.

waists. The object of the game is to throw
a dead calf or goat carcass across a goal line.
Before the game, the carcass is beheaded,
its legs cut off at the knee, and its entrails
removed. It is then soaked in cold water for 24
hours to make it tough. A game of *buzkashi*
may last as long as a week. Wrestling matches
in which the participants prove their strength

▲ These men on horseback are playing *buzkashi*.
The man in red is carrying the animal carcass that
has to be thrown across the goal line.

accompany the game. *Buzkashi* is a very fast
game, and players are often injured. Other
sports that are popular in the country are
soccer and snowboarding.

Focus on: Kite Flying

The people of Afghanistan like to fly kites.
Kite flying in Afghanistan is not like kite flying
anywhere else. In the sport of *Gudiparan bazi*
(meaning "flying doll"), people fly kites with
strings coated with crushed glass; using these
strings, they try to cut the string of an opponent's
kite and set it free. Kites in Afghanistan come in
all sizes, from miniature to as big as a person.

They are made of thin paper and bamboo. The
string is very important, and coating it in ground
glass is a very complicated operation that often
involves severe cuts to the fingers. The wire
is then wound around a drum. Most areas in
a neighborhood have a *sharti*, or kite flying
champion. The Taliban banned kite flying,
but it has recently been reintroduced.

▶ This woman is making colorful kites for the traditional sport of kite flying.

TOURISM

In the nineteenth and early twentieth centuries, many travelers came to Afghanistan. The author Robert Byron, who, in 1933, wrote *The Road to Oxiana* about his travels in the region, said that the garden where he stayed in Kabul was "too pleasant to leave, full of sweet williams, Canterbury bells, and columbines, planted among the lawns and terraces and shady arbors; it might be England until one notices the purple mountain behind the big white house."

It is obvious that, with its rugged mountains and ancient treasures, Afghanistan would be a popular destination for tourists if it were not for war. Its first national park, Band-e-Amir, has several lakes of crystal-clear water, surrounded by towering red cliffs. Urial, a type of wild sheep, and ibex, or wild goats, live in the park. Although the park is a UNESCO World Heritage Site, it remains heavily planted with landmines from 2001, when it was the frontline between the Taliban and those opposing them.

The Kole Hashmat Khan wetland on the outskirts of Kabul was declared a waterfowl reserve by King Zahir Shah in the 1930s. In the 1960s, it supported tens of thousands of ducks, as well as wintering and migratory birds. But this wetland has not been protected. Many internally displaced people live in it, and its bird life has declined.

In the 1970s, tourism in Afghanistan reached its peak, with about 90,000 visitors a year making a significant contribution to the country's earnings. Even under the Taliban, there was a Minister of Tourism, although the Taliban's strict version of Islam did not

 Did You Know?

Some children in Afghanistan had a unique way of marking the UN's "Make Poverty History" campaign. In September 2005, more than 300 Afghan children flew white kites to draw the attention of world leaders.

encourage tourists to visit. Today, a few intrepid visitors are making their way to Afghanistan, but their safety is not guaranteed. Some popular travel guides now include a section on Afghanistan. In spite of this, the United States government Web site warns that the country is currently too dangerous for U.S. citizens to visit. Most foreigners in Afghanistan today are aid workers or journalists rather than tourists.

Tourism in Afghanistan

- ◻ Tourist arrivals, millions: not available
- ◻ Earnings from tourism in U.S.$: not available
- ◻ Tourism as % foreign earnings: not available
- ◻ Tourist departures, millions: not available
- ◻ Expenditure on tourism in U.S.$: 1,000,000

Source: World Bank

◀ The grounds and mosque of Baghe Babur date back to 1638. This site in Kabul has recently been reopened. Afghanistan has many beautiful ancient buildings like this that may become popular with tourists in the future.

Focus on: Kabul Zoo

Humans suffered during the years of war in Afghanistan, and so did the animals at Kabul Zoo. The zoo used to have 50 species of birds and animals. The number of species in the zoo dropped to 16 during the war years, when it was closed. With the help of the World Society for the Prevention of Cruelty to Animals, the Kabul Zoo has reopened. Today, it has 100 animals, mostly from Afghanistan itself, and an educational program for children. As one of the few places of entertainment in the city, the zoo attracts up to 5,000 visitors during weekends. Concerns were expressed by some of the Kabul Zoo's visitors about the treatment of the zoo animals when a bear and a deer died after being fed chewing tobacco.

CHAPTER 13

Environment and Conservation

A fghanistan's environment is harsh. The arid land and long, cold winters make it difficult for people, plants, or animals to survive. In 2,000 B.C., the country was covered with cedar-rich forests. Over the years, however, its people were forced to cut down the forests for fuel and in order to make a living, and their animals overgrazed the already fragile fields. As a result, the country's soil has been eroded by water and wind. The effects of irrigation, which has been practiced in Afghanistan over many years, have made much of the country's land that might be suitable for cultivation—which, at most, covers only 12 percent of its area—too salty for use. Only 6 percent of the country's land is currently being used for farming.

POLLUTION AND WATER SHORTAGE

Water in Afghanistan is scarce and often polluted by chemicals and waste. Most of its cities do not have regular garbage collection, resulting in health hazards and sometimes groundwater pollution. Many deep wells have been drilled, and these wells affect groundwater levels, including levels in the traditional *karez* system of underground water canals.

? Did You Know?

Although it does not have much industry of its own, Kabul suffers from smog. Kabul's smog problem results partly from the amount of firewood burned in a city with few other sources of light, heat, or cooking fuel and partly from vehicle emissions. Industrial parks in Iran, Turkmenistan, and Uzbekistan also pump out emissions that pollute the air in Kabul.

◀ A woman and two children draw water from a standpipe in a street. Many Afghan people have no access to clean water.

Between 1998 and 2002, four years of drought resulted in the Helmand River running as much as 98 percent below its annual average. A United Nations study in 2002 found that more than 99 percent of the Sistan wetlands, a critically important haven for waterfowl, had become completely dry. In the 1970s, before the Soviet invasion, Afghanistan's government, with the help of the UN and other agencies, began to address some of these problems. The country today has seven protected areas, though they cover less than 1 percent of the land.

PLANTS AND TREES

Before the years of war, forest lands amounted to about 5 million acres (about 2 million hectares), or about 4.5 percent of the country in eastern and southeastern Afghanistan. Since 1979, about 33 percent of the country's forests have disappeared. Less than 2 percent of the

Focus on: Landmines in Afghanistan

There are between five million and seven million landmines planted in Afghanistan. Most of them were planted during the Soviet occupation. Up to 150 people a month are injured by landmines, and more than 200,000 have been killed or injured by landmines over the past two decades. Many of these victims are children, including young shepherds tending sheep. In May 2006, Afghanistan's government reported that it had destroyed 65,973 stockpiled landmines since signing the Mine Ban Treaty in 2002. It is also

slowly clearing existing landmines. So far, 7,000 Afghans have been trained in the dangerous work of demining. Many warlords and militias, however, still possess landmines, as do nearby countries such as Myanmar (Burma), India, Nepal, and Pakistan. Laws have been passed to give landmine victims free medical care.

▼ A man searches for unexploded landmines. This is a delicate and dangerous job. Clearing Afghanistan of landmines will take many years.

country is now forested. Trees include various kinds of evergreens (including some ancient cedars), oaks, poplars, wild hazelnuts, almonds, and pistachios. In the northern steppes and the southwestern deserts, plants such as camel thorn, locoweed, spiny restharrow, mimosa, and wormwood (a variety of sagebrush) flourish, in spite the harsh conditions.

ANIMALS AND BIRDS

More than 100 types of mammals manage to live in Afghanistan. Some of them, such as the goitered gazelle, leopard, snow leopard, markor goat, and Bactrian deer, are in danger of dying out. Other wild animals living in Afghanistan include Marco Polo sheep, ibex, bears, wolves, foxes, hyenas, jackals, mongooses, wild boars, hedgehogs, shrews, hares, mouse hares, bats, and a variety of rodents. The country has more than 380 bird species. Flamingos and other water birds breed in the lake areas south and east of Ghazni. Ducks and partridge are also common. All birds in the country are hunted widely, and many are in serious danger of dying out, especially the Siberian crane.

CONSERVATION

In 2002, the Loya Jirga set up the Ministry for Irrigation, Water Resources, and Environment (MIWRE) to take the lead in ensuring that care for the environment was a part of the reconstruction process. Some of the money designated for Afghanistan by the international community is being used for the conservation of wildlife and the environment. The Asian Development Bank (ADB), for example, has promised about U.S.$1.8 million to protect plant and animal life in certain regions. The United Nations Environment Program (UNEP), together with the European Commission and MIWRE, has promised U.S.$5.15 million to support the rehabilitation of the country's environment. The United Nations Millennium Development goals for Afghanistan include helping to make sure that any development that

Environmental and Conservation Data

- Forested area as % total land area: 0.04
- Protected area as % total land area: 0.3
- Number of protected areas: 7

SPECIES DIVERSITY

Category	Known species	Threatened species
Mammals	119	13
Breeding birds	181	11
Reptiles	109	1
Amphibians	7	1
Fish	115	n/a
Plants	4,000	1

Source: World Resources Institute

◀ The snow leopard is one of the most endangered mammals in Afghanistan and in the world.

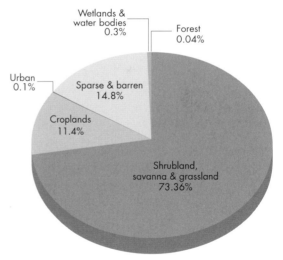

◀ A young boy sells firewood from the back of his bike on the outskirts of Kabul. Many poor families have no choice but to burn precious wood for fuel.

occurs in the country does not destroy the environment and helping to reverse the loss of environmental resources. In January 2006, the government enacted Afghanistan's first environmental legislation, which aims to protect and conserve wildlife, waterways, and forests.

In spite of promises of money, repairing the country's ravaged environment may take a long time. When the country's people have so little, protecting the environment for future generations comes second to the battle for daily survival—even if this includes cutting down precious trees. Many people in Afghanistan sell firewood so that their children can eat.

Wetlands & water bodies 0.3%

Forest 0.04%

Urban 0.1%

Sparse & barren 14.8%

Croplands 11.4%

Shrubland, savanna & grassland 73.36%

▲ Types of habitat

Did You Know?

The large, longhaired, silky Afghan hound comes from Afghanistan! Afghan hounds were brought to Britain in the nineteenth century.

Did You Know?

In 1978, Afghanistan had 70 Siberian cranes. By 2006, according to Society for Afghanistan's Viable Environment (SAVE), the country had only three Siberian cranes left—one pair with a chick.

Future Challenges

Afghanistan faces many challenges. It remains a country in conflict. Rebuilding, forging political stability and security, reducing poverty, raising life expectancy, improving conditions for women, and combating the drug trade are all among the important—and difficult—challenges facing the country. The country's rate of violent crime is higher today than at any time since 2001. The gap between rich and poor is increasing, particularly in Kabul, where some people are making lots of money. Many refugees are returning from the West and making big contributions to society, but they also bring different perspectives and are usually richer than those Afghans who remained in the country. These factors can cause tensions between returning Afghans and those who lived in the country through its years of war.

THE STRUGGLE FOR CONTROL

Afghanistan's government is not in control of the parts of the country ruled by the warlords, and Taliban fighters remain in the mountains and remote areas. Osama bin Laden and other Al-Qaeda leaders have still not been found, in spite of the thousands of foreign troops in the country looking for them. But there are some signs of hope. The country's new government is in place, with a national parliament and legal system. Many people have been able to vote for the first time in their lives. Women are slowly returning to public life, though many face intimidation and violence for doing so. Four million students are back in school. Health care is improving. Immunization campaigns, for example, have caused the number of polio and measles cases in the country to drop.

▶ Since the fall of the Taliban, girls in Afghanistan are able to enjoy playing games openly. Although the Taliban is no longer in power, however, it still exists and poses a threat.

◀ British soldiers of the NATO-led International Security and Assistance Force (ISAF) patrol the streets of Kabul in July 2006.

More than U.S.$852 million have been pledged to the Afghanistan Reconstruction Trust Fund (ARTF) by 24 donor countries. If things are to improve, all the money promised needs to be delivered. Infrastructure must be improved so that transportation systems function and electricity and clean water are delivered to the people. Education and health also need support and investment. The country needs to be made safe enough for Afghan refugees to return, and the economy needs to become strong enough for them to be able to make a living again.

Above all, the Afghan people need to own what is happening in their country—from the government to local communities. This is not easy, because the country has so many problems, and international aid and foreign governments play such important roles. A conference in London in February 2006 attended by representatives from almost 70 countries backed a peace plan and pledged resources to rebuild the country. All agree that this will take time and will not be an easy task.

 Did You Know?

In Kabul, there is a new shopping mall and a five-star hotel.. In this hotel, most rooms cost U.S.$250 a night, and the presidential suite costs U.S.$1,200 a night.

Focus on: Child Soldiers

Many boys fought in Afghanistan's wars, both for the Taliban and against them. A UNICEF program, started in February 2004, has so far helped 4,000 of these young people to find their way back into employment and normal life. With the help of local people, these boys can learn skills such as animal husbandry, tailoring, masonry, car repair, and carpentry. They are also given medical checks and educational opportunities. Each of these former child soldier signs a pledge in which he agrees to help with the reconstruction of his country and not to return to fighting.

Time Line

329 B.C. Alexander the Great conquers Afghanistan and Persia.

A.D. 100 Kushan Buddhist Empire.

400 White Huns invade from the north and destroy Buddhist culture.

530 Persians gain control of the whole of Afghanistan.

650–1030 Islamic era established by invading Arabs. Ghaznavid and Ghorid dynasties continue after the Arabs leave.

1219–1221 Genghis Khan invades.

1370 Tamerlane conquers Afghanistan.

1330? Ghorid dynasty reestablishes itself.

1504–1419 Babur, a descendant of Timur and founder of the Moghul dynasty, takes control of Kabul.

1520 Afghanistan becomes part of the Moghul Empire, established in India under Timur's successors.

1550 Persian Empire takes over in the West.

1613–1689 Khushhal Khan Khattak, an Afghan warrior poet, starts an uprising against the Moghul government.

1725 Mir Mahmud invades Persia.

1735 Persia drives back Mahmud and retakes Kandahar.

1750–1775 Afghans liberate Kandahar and drive the Moghuls back into India. Ahmad Shah Durrani establishes the Kingdom of Afghanistan.

1820s Britain and Russia both want control of central Asia.

1839–1842 First Afghan War between British and Afghans.

1878 Second Afghan War. Khyber and Pischin concede to the British.

1880 Battle of Maiwand. Abdul Rahman Khan takes the throne with the help of Britain, which withdraws but retains the power to handle foreign relations.

1920–1921 Third Afghan War. Afghanistan gains independence from Britain.

1930–1933 Nadir Khan takes the throne and founds a dynasty that rules until 1978.

1940 Mohammed Zahir Shah declares Afghanistan neutral in World War II; the kingdom retreats into isolation.

1953 Daoud Khan becomes prime minister.

1959 Women are allowed to enroll at universities and to join the workforce.

1963 Zahir Shah usurps Daoud and gives limited powers to a parliament.

1973 Zahir Shah's government is overthrown in a coup headed by his cousin Daoud Khan, who abolishes the monarchy and declares himself president of the republic.

1978 Communist coup. Daoud is killed and Nur Mohammed Taraki is made president. Taraki signs a treaty of friendship with the Soviet Union. The Afghan mujahideen movement is born.

1979 Soviet Army massacres peasants. The U.S. ambassador and Taraki are killed. Babrak Karmal takes power. The Soviet Union invades to fight the mujahideen and support Karmal. Covert CIA aid to mujahideen begins. Millions of Afghans flee to refugee camps in Pakistan.

1980–1986 CIA provides $2 billion in military aid to mujahideen, who also turn to the opium trade to fund their war.

1987 Soviets install KGB-trained secret police chief Mohammed Najibullah, who becomes president.

1988–1989 Peace accords signed in Geneva. Soviet Union withdraws. Mujahideen continue to fight against Najibullah.

1992 Mujahideen take control of Kabul and declare an Islamic state under Burhanuddin Rabbani.

1994 Founding of the Taliban.

1996 The Taliban forces President Rabbani and his government out of Kabul and execute Najibullah. Taliban offers refuge to Osama bin Laden.

1999 United Nations Security Council imposes sanctions.

2001 September 11 terrorist attacks on the United States. The United States and its allies overthrow the Taliban to capture bin Laden and disrupt Al-Qaeda. The Bonn Agreement establishes an interim government with Hamid Karzai as its president.

2004 Afghanistan's first presidential election since 1969. Hamid Karzai is elected.

2005 Parliamentary elections are held.

May 2006 Several people are killed by a U.S. military vehicle; violent protests against the United States take place in Kabul.

May–June 2006 Battles between Taliban fighters and Afghan and coalition forces in Afghanistan's south.

July 2006–present NATO troops take over leadership of military operations in the south. Fighting against the Taliban continues.

September 2006 Safia Hama Jan, a leading women's rights figure and outspoken critic of the Taliban, is murdered on the streets of Kandahar.

Glossary

assassination killing of a person for political reasons

burqa a garment that covers the whole of a woman's body and face, leaving only a mesh panel for the eyes

Central Intelligence Agency (CIA) the intelligence agency of the United States

coalition an alliance of different countries or parties who agree to work or fight together

communism a political system in which power resides with a single party that controls all economic activities and provides services

controversy an argument or debate, especially one carried on in public or in the media

coup the overthrow of a ruler of a country often, but not always, by the military

covertly secretly

democracy a political system in which each adult person has the right to vote and government is made up of elected representatives

ethnic having to do with a group of people who share a cultural and historical tradition, often associated with race, nationality, or religion

European Commission the branch of the governing body of the European Union (EU) that carries out its laws and administers some of its money

European Union a union of 25 countries that aims to improve political, economic, and social cooperation

gender the behaviors and cultural roles associated with being male or female

Gross Domestic Product (GDP) the total market value of goods and services in a country

internally displaced persons people who have had to leave their homes out of fear of persecution or because of a natural disaster and who live somewhere else within their own countries

International Monetary Fund (IMF) a United Nations agency that aims to promote trade and increase growth by stabilizing exchange rates

Islamist a person who believes that government and society should follow Islamic law

jurisprudence a system of law

Loya Jirga the traditional governing Grand Council of Afghanistan

madrassa an Islamic school where the Koran is taught by rote

militia an armed group that is usually independent and not connected to a government

mujahideen guerrilla fighters in an Islamic country

mullah an Islamic religious teacher

nomad a member of a people who do not live in one place and usually moves around within a certain area

nomadic frequently moving from place to place

North Atlantic Treaty Organization (NATO) the military alliance of the United States and several European countries formed after World War II with the initial aim of preventing the Soviet Union from invading Europe

plateau a flat expanse of land at a high altitude

puppet king a leader who has little real power and is usually controlled by another country

refugee someone who has been forced to leave his or her home country out of fear of danger or persecution on account of race, religion, nationality, membership in a particular social group, or political opinion

Sharia the Islamic code of law based on the Koran

Shi'a Muslims Muslims who believe that religious authority lies with a direct descent of the Prophet Muhammad

steppes vast, flat, treeless plains that are usually covered in grass

Sunni Muslims Muslims who believe that religious authority must lie with the person chosen by the religious community as their leader; Sunnis accept the first four caliphs as the righful successors to the Prophet Muhammad

tectonic plate one of the pieces of Earth's crust that floats on its mantle

terrorists people who use violence, usually against civilians, to scare others into giving in to their political demands

tribe families, clans, or other groups who share a common ancestry and culture

United Nations an organization founded at the end of World War II with the aim of preventing future wars

United Nations Children's Fund (UNICEF) the United Nations organization that is responsible for children all over the world

World Bank an international organization that lends money to poor countries

World Health Organization (WHO) the United Nations organization that promotes health around the world

Zoroastrianism the religion founded by Zoroaster in the tenth century B.C. that is based on the idea of conflict between good and evil and has a particular reverence for fire

Further Information

BOOKS TO READ

Abrams, Dennis. *Hamid Karzai*
(Modern World Leaders).
Chelsea House, 2007.

Boaz, John. *The U.S. Attack on
Afghanistan* (At Issue in History).
Greenhaven Press, 2005.

Greenblatt, Miriam. *Afghanistan*
(Enchantment of the World).
Children's Press, 2003.

Gritzner, Jeffrey and John F. Shroder.
Afghanistan (Modern World Nations).
Chelsea House, 2006.

Kazem, Halima. *Afghanistan*
(Countries of the World).
Gareth Stevens, 2002.

Lohfelm, Bill. *Osama bin Laden*
(Heroes and Villains).
Lucent Books, 2003.

Streissguth, Thomas (editor).
Afghanistan (The History of
Nations). Greenhaven Press, 2005).

USEFUL WEB SITES

Afghanistan - Country in Crisis
www.unicef.org/emerg/afghanistan/index.html

*Afghanistan - Images from the Harrison Forman
Collection*
www.uwm.edu/Library/digilib/afghan/

CIA World Factbook: Afghanistan
www.cia.gov/cia/publications/factbook/
geos/af.html

Cool Planet: Afghanistan
www.oxfam.org.uk/coolplanet/kidsweb/
world/afghan/index.htm

Scholastic News: Kids in Afghanistan
www.teacher.scholastic.com/scholasticnews/inde
pth/afghanistan_kids/

Understanding Afghanistan: Land in Crisis
www.nationalgeographic.com/landincrisis/

Publisher's note to educators and parents: Our editors have
carefully reviewed these Web sites to ensure that they are
suitable for children. Many Web sites change frequently,
however, and we cannot guarantee that a site's future
contents will continue to meet our high standards of quality
and educational value. Be advised that children should
be closely supervised whenever they access the Internet.

Index

Page numbers in **bold** indicate pictures.

About the Author

Nikki van der Gaag is a freelance writer, editor, and evaluator on development issues. She has held senior editorial posts in the voluntary and not-for-profit sector. She was editorial director at the Panos Institute, coeditor of *New Internationalist* magazine, and Education Publications Manager with Oxfam GB.